A LITTLE NOTE FROM ME TO YOU

Hey there.

My name is Billie-Girl, and I live in the Bahamas. It is beautiful here. The sun shines most days, and it's usually warm. I have fun doggy friends, loving humans, and strange new creatures to discover every day. We go on lots of island adventures, and I watch the sun rise over the ocean every morning. Each sunrise reminds me of how lucky I am and how much I have to be thankful for. I didn't always live here, you see, and life wasn't always this good. In fact, at first, mine was a pretty rough life. Sometimes you gotta go through the rough times, though, to get to the good part.

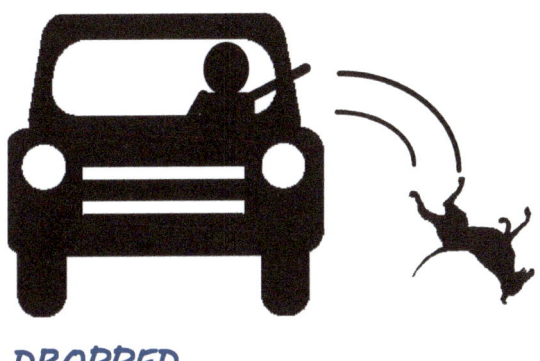

DROPPED

Pavement & taillights. That is my first memory...and cold. Pavement, taillights, and cold. I still don't know WHY my first humans didn't want me, or WHY they decided to throw me from a moving car, or even WHY they couldn't at least wait until it was warm outside. I didn't have much time then to spend on wondering "WHY". A few moments after I was dropped onto the road a huge truck came speeding down the mountainside blasting his horn at me.

"MOVE!! MOVE!!! MOVE!!!"
It seemed to say.
More cars followed, their horns all blaring the same thing.
"MOVE!!!" I was a smart puppy, so I moved. I ran toward the forest beside the highway, and discovered that I'd injured one of my back legs when I hit the pavement. Every footstep hurt, but I had to keep running. It seems like that's all I did for the next couple of weeks: Run. Running hurt, but at least when I ran I was warm. (The Blue Ridge Mountains are cold in January.) Once I found food on the ground outside of a big building. Some humans saw me eating it, though and threw rocks at me. "Get out of here you no-good mutt!" I don't know WHY they were so

angry at me and wanted to hurt me. I kept running. I ran past houses, through half-frozen streams, through the snow, into the woods, down a hill, into a ditch, back up a hill, and onto pavement...**SCREECH!!!** The tires of a big car screamed at me as the driver slammed on the brakes. I started to run again, but a pain, sharper than before, shot up my hurt leg and I let out a yelp. I heard a soft voice come from the car that I'd run in front of. "Here puppy. Come little one." I looked at the human, not sure if I should trust her or not. What if she just wanted to hurt me like the other humans? She'd left the car door open behind her, and I could feel the heater's warm air from all the way across the road. I could smell something inside the car that made my stomach growl so loud it scared me. I ran past the human and jumped into the warm, soft seat next to where she had been sitting. A white square box sat on the floor of the car. I started drooling at the smell of fresh hot bread, melted cheese, juicy meats, and more cheese. I didn't notice the human approaching until she closed the car door. I stared at her, and she stared at me. Her hand came toward me, and I remembered the humans who tried to hurt me when I ate before. I growled and showed her my teeth and tried to figure out how I was going to escape. She opened the box on the floor, and I nearly swooned when the

delicious smelling steam rose up from the box. "Want a piece of pizza, little girl?" If pizza was the stuff in the white box, then YES, PLEASE! I couldn't stop my tail from wagging a little. She lifted a slice of gooey, melty, meaty goodness and put it in front of me. I decided right then and there that pizza is the most wonderful thing that humans have EVER done. I laid down to savor a second slice and yelped when my weight fell on my bad leg. "Poor little girl. Looks like you broke your leg. It just so happens I work at a hospital. Let's see if we can't get you looked at before everyone gets there. Thank goodness for all this snow." We got to the hospital place, and the human (Mel, she called herself) wrapped me in a big soft blanket, and carried me into a side door. I heard her talking to other humans. "...just found her in the road...nearly starved to death, and I think her leg is broken. I just want to x-ray it so I know where to put the splint. I'll have her in and out before anyone knows. Just run the machine for me." Mel took me into a room and held me on a table while another human went

into a small room and pushed
buttons. The other human left
and then came back a few
minutes later. "Dr. Frinkel says
this patient has several very
serious conditions. First of all,
one of their legs is deformed
and looks very much like a dog's
leg. Secondly, their dog leg is
very badly broken. He's sending
an ER tech to help set the
human patient's dog leg. Then he
says get this patient out of here
before we all get fired."

Things moved fast after that.
Someone wearing green came
into the room and pulled on my
leg while the Mel strapped a
stick to it and wrapped cloth
around and around and around. A
man in a suit came in and said
that the patient's condition was
worse than he'd feared.

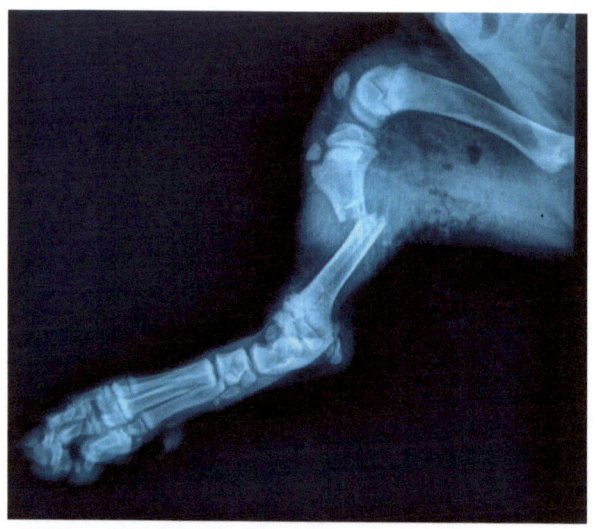

"The dog leg syndrome has spread." He told the Mel to get me to a veterinarian and take the x-rays with her. After that the Mel and I went to another hospital place and they put a hard case around my leg that covered from my foot up to my hip. They gave me shots, which I didn't like, but then the Mel gave me more pizza, so it was ok. "Come on, Billie-Girl. Let's get you home." I went to sleep as we drove back down the mountain where she'd found me, warm and full of food for the first time in 2 weeks.

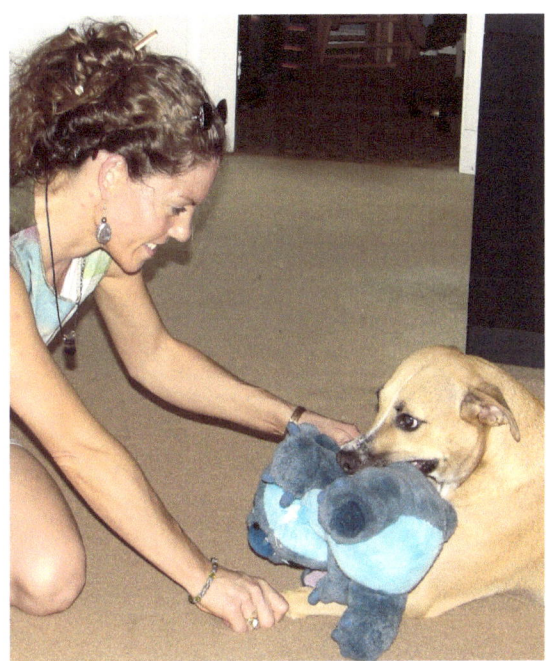

MOUNTAIN MUTTS

I stayed with the Mel, and when my leg had healed enough, she said she wanted to introduce me to my new family. We went outside to a fenced-in yard with a little log cabin inside of it. Confused I looked up at the Mel and then back at the little house. "Crystal! Sugar-Bear! Come meet your little sister, Billie-Girl." A loud thumping and bumping and clanging and banging erupted from the tiny cabin as two HUGE dog-like creatures both tried to squeeze through a tiny doorway at the same time. One was easily 3 times my size. Her fluffy fur was so light a grey that it was almost white. I learned that this was Crystal. The other one, Sugar-Bear, was more than twice her size and looked like a Grizzly Bear. They barked & woofed and howled & yipped at me in welcome. The Mel and I went into their yard, and Mel set me on the ground. The giant St. Bernard/Mastiff, Sugar-Bear, bounced around like there were springs in her legs and the Timberwolf/Husky, Crystal, ran around me in circles. "We're so glad you're better. We can't wait to play with you!" They seemed to say. Let me tell you, I felt the exact same way. My tail was wagging so hard my whole body wagged! I had a family and they loved me!

14

THE GREAT WAR

After meeting Crystal and Sugar-Bear, I wanted to be with them all the time. I hated being kept inside the house while the Mel went to work during the day. She said that I was still not healed enough to be with Crystal and Sugar-Bear full time.
One of the days that I was locked inside the house...AGAIN...Crystal and Sugar-Bear started barking and howling up a storm. Something was near the house that had come from the woods. I sniffed around the door and, sure enough, I could smell something. I didn't know what it was, but it definitely smelled like it needed to be chased. I tried to get out of the door.

I scratched at it and jumped on it and howled. No luck. Still locked inside! I got so mad that I couldn't get outside and chase that thing. I could hear it in the Mel's herb garden munching away, and I couldn't get out there to make it go! I turned my food bowl over and pulled down the gate that the Mel put up to keep me away from certain parts of the house. I went into a room with a fireplace and there found a big white furry rug on the floor. It smelled similar to the thing that was outside! It wasn't moving or doing anything, but I just knew it would wait until I wasn't looking and jump up and start eating things inside, just like the one outside was!

The Mel worked hard on her little house, and I sure wasn't going to let this demented flat fur monster eat it all! What if it didn't stop at eating plants and carpet and furniture and candles?! What if it got a taste for me or the Mel or my new doggy family? A righteous fury filled me and I knew I had to do what I had to do. I had to save my family from the bloodthirsty Flat Fur Monster! I circled around it several times to confuse it, and when I was sure it didn't know from which way I would attack, I leapt onto it and sank my teeth into it. Knowing that this fight could make a mess I drug the Flat Fur Monster into the kitchen onto the hard floor. I held it with my paws and ripped at it with my teeth, tearing pieces out of it. It wasn't fighting back, but I knew that was all part of its act. As soon as I turned around it would creep up on me and get me! My fury was now turning to fear as I thought about what the Flat Fur Monster would do to me. I tore it into millions of tiny pieces and then dragged the pieces all around the house to keep it from putting itself back together. I laid down exhausted and thought of how pleased the Mel would be that I had protected everyone from the Flat Fur Monster. I got thinking about all those small pieces that I had scattered around the house. What if they hid themselves in the laundry that was sitting folded on the couch? They would get the Mel and she wouldn't even know what it was! Frantic, I pulled all the clothes off of the couch, pawing through shirts, socks, and pants in search of tiny Flat Fur Monsters. I couldn't find them, but I thought the prudent thing to do, just in case, was to drag each piece of clothing to separate places in the house. I laid down panting. No more Flat Fur Monster to worry about. I rested for what may have been minutes or days, I don't know. A soft rustling awoke me, though. Nose to the floor I searched for the source of the sound. After what felt like hours I discovered the sound was coming from one of the plants that the Mel kept on the kitchen counter. Its leaves were softly waving in a breeze coming from the ceiling. I watched it suspiciously. It looked like the perfect place for tiny pieces of the Flat Fur Monster to hide. Well, to make a very long story short, The Battle of The Flat Fur Monster raged throughout the day.

 I finally had obliterated all hiding places for the Flat Fur Monster's evil offspring, and jumped up onto the Mel's bed to rest and guard against enemy resurgence.

I MEET A STRANGER

After "The Great War" was fought I slept like the dead. (Protecting Home and Family is tiring work, after all.) I didn't hear the back door open or the soft footsteps that stopped in the kitchen. I awoke to the sound of an unfamiliar voice coming from far off in the house. "Mel, I think someone broke in. The house is completely trashed. Your kitchen plants are all over the place, and your sheepskin looks like it went through a blender. Your laundry is EVERYWHERE! Huh? Is what puppy ok...I don't see a puppy. Alright, stay on the phone with me while I check the rest of the house. No, don't call the cops yet."

I heard the voice and footsteps coming down the hallway and burrowed behind the pillows on the Mel's bed. The voice stopped in the doorway, and I peeked out between the pillows. "I think I found her; that, or your pillow grew a tail and is wagging it. What a cutie! No worries, we'll have a talk while I get this all cleaned up. Billie-Girl? Ok."

This new human called herself "Sarah", and I don't think she liked me at first. She picked up pieces of the Flat-Fur-Monster, and re-folded the clothes that had been possible hiding places for it. The plants that had conspired with the Flat-Fur-Monster were swept up and deposited outside, and the candles that had been knocked over and broken during the most heated part of the battle were thrown into the trash bin. I regretted the candles, but in any skirmish there is collateral damage. It's a sad fact of war. Throughout the clean-up she muttered uncomplimentary things and threw dirty looks at me as she swept. When all signs of the battle had been cleared away and order re-stored, the Sarah flopped down on the couch and rested while watching the picture box. I laid on the floor watching her until, finally, she patted the couch next to her and said, "Well, come on then." I jumped up and wedged myself between her and the back of the sofa. I was glad of the warmth and comfort provided by human touch after the horrors of the day. The Sarah idly stroked behind my ears, and I slowly relaxed against her and fell into a deep sleep.

A PERSON OF MY OWN

 Even though I was very happy with the Mel, a part of me knew I had just found My Person. Sarah must've felt this connection as well, because when she left to "go up to the mountains" she took me with her. From then on I was Hers and she was Mine.

Over the next few years there were wonderful times. We hiked through the fields and along streams in the mountains of West Virginia.

We drove into The City to meet friends of Sarah's and sat outside at restaurants. I was allowed to lie under the table, and the Waitress would "accidentally" drop pieces of food in front of me from the plates she carried away after people finished eating.

We lived with Sarah's family, and we all sat together at night to eat dinner or watch shows in the picture box.

Sometimes we went back to visit the Mel and Crystal and Sugar-Bear. Those were good times.

There were some rough times too. Sarah's family had a herd of dogs that were called "Corgis". I didn't like them.

Though loving and loyal to their humans, they hated any animal that was "Un-Corgi". When everyone left during the day to go to work, if The Corgis were able to escape from their part of the house, they would hunt me down and take turns tormenting me. To this day, one of my ears still doesn't stand up straight from a Corgi-inflicted injury. They were good to their humans, though.

Days, weeks, and months passed, and so did some of the animals around the farm.

We were all sad when a furred family member passed, but before long a new animal would come along who needed help (just like I did). Sarah and her family would welcome them into the family and care for them as they were able. Some of them stayed and some went on to live with Sarah's Sisters, Brothers, or friends.

WE FIND OUR THIRD

In time, Sarah eventually met Her Person, and we went to live with him near The City. It didn't take me long to understand why she was so taken with this new person, Butch. I quickly came to regard Him as Mine as well. He and I rode in boats, fished off of the marina docks, and He took me on something called a 'jet ski'. It was like a small boat that went REALLY fast. I loved it! (To any dogs out there who are reading this: If your humans do not have a 'jet ski', I highly recommend asking them to get one for you. They are an invention almost as wonderful as Pizza.)

Things were looking Up.
Sarah was Happy. I was Happy,
and Our Butch was Happy.

Life was Good. .

FROM THERE TO HERE

That all seems like it was forever ago, or maybe just yesterday. We had many adventures together on the Great Potomac River and I made many new friends. Our greatest adventure yet, our move to The Bahamas, was fast approaching, but that is a tail...I mean tale for another time. Until then, dear Friends, my advice to you is to love each other and love your furry family members. Treat us well, and care for those of us whom others have not treated well. We will repay you with undying devotion and infinite love. Until The Next Time,

Billie-Girl

Look for Billie-Girl's next big adventure:

From There To Here

Visit Billie-Girl Online!

http://billiegirltheislanddog.blogspot.com

www.ingramcontent.com/pod-product-compliance
Lightning Source LLC
Chambersburg PA
CBHW041527090426
42736CB00035B/35